Praise for *The Wells of Venice*

"The elegance of Jefferson Holdridge's poems is born out of the natural cadence of language, which he wisely assumes, and his communion with a city he loves: Venice. Tensions lead to resolutions that are organic to each scene and to the characters, historical and contemporary, who contribute to his love. . . . Conflict yields to beauty, angst to grace: enduring antidotes to the ennui of our times."

— Sofia M. Starnes,
Virginia Poet Laureate Emerita

"Holdridge captures in exact language those moments when the imaginative audacity that is Venice is somehow chastened by the pressure of a felt and actual experience. This is an art which begins in traditional metaphor but returns us to a radical realism — fragile, beautiful, and defiant of time's erosions. Here are poems of luminous elegance, immaculate as cut glass yet true to the impure elements out of which all lovely things are made. They offer a response to a dreamlike city that is at once urgently personal and serenely historical."

— Declan Kiberd, author of *Inventing Ireland: The Literature of the Modern Nation*

"It's here, the cornucopia effect: relentless patience, tranquil urgency, radical relevance; the architectural petulance of the Twin Towers reduced to rubble, zone zero, the goose-stepping march of history; will Venice also fall? Epoch of change or change of epoch? The transience of magnificence, brittleness of beauty; 'Jerusalem, Jerusalem, not a stone will remain upon stone.' Craftsmanship: compelling rhythms and reflections, rhymes subtle, discreet, inevitable. The unflinching poetic gaze, refusing to settle for the apparent, the implacable pursuit of the underlying — what lies under and doesn't lie or disappoint — piercing the eternal now. Nothingness fails to prevail. Being irresistibly is."

— COLUM POWER, AUTHOR OF *JAMES JOYCE'S CATHOLIC CATEGORIES*

"Jefferson Holdridge is a poet par excellence, yet his poems — be they short lyrics or extended meditations on historical figures and artworks — are more than structures of 'purposeless beauty.' When the poet writes, 'Imagine a city you once called home,' we better show up ready to follow him down every nook and cranny, prepared 'for any tremor or rising tide.' Replete with wisdom and wonder, Holdridge's work is a testament to the indefatigability of the human spirit."

— PIOTR FLORCZYK, AUTHOR OF *EAST & WEST* AND *FROM THE ANNALS OF KRAKÓW*

THE WELLS OF VENICE

THE WELLS OF VENICE

Poems

Jefferson Holdridge

RESOURCE *Publications* • Eugene, Oregon

THE WELLS OF VENICE
Poems

Cover Image: Sargent, John Singer
Campo Sant' Agnese, Venice
ca. 1882
Oil on canvas
18 in. x 25 5/8 in. (45.7 cm x 65.1 cm)
with permission from the Davis Museum at Wellesley College, Wellesley, MA

Resource Publications
An Imprint of Wipf and Stock Publishers
199 W. 8th Ave., Suite 3
Eugene, OR 97401

www.wipfandstock.com

PAPERBACK ISBN: 978-1-7252-8739-6
HARDCOVER ISBN: 978-1-7252-8738-9
EBOOK ISBN: 978-1-7252-8740-2

Manufactured in the U.S.A. 11/19/20

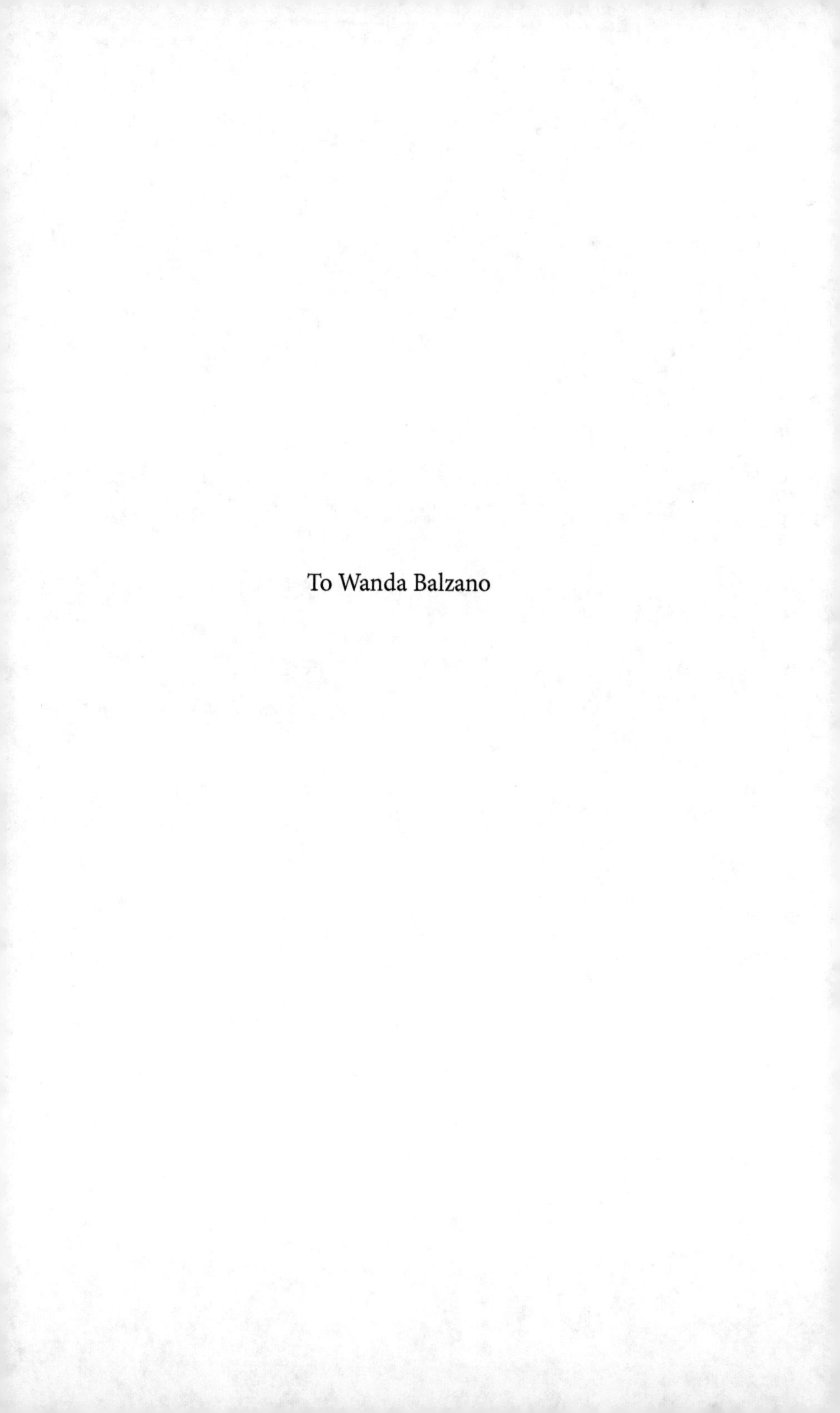

To Wanda Balzano

Contents

Acknowledgments

I WOULD LIKE TO thank friends and colleagues in Venice: Shaul Bassi, Agnese Chiari, Roberta Cimarosti, Laura Graziano, Massimo Basso, Cheti Bettio, and Michela Pitteri whose knowledge of Venetian literature and art, and whose love for the city enabled this book at every step of the way in the years from 2007–2018 in which for various semesters I was at Casa Artom (Wake Forest University's house in Venice). I would also like to thank the many other Venetians I met along the way, especially those parents and their children who welcomed my family into their lives. *Grazie mille e non vedo l'ora di rivedervi.*

Also, I would like to thank those at Wake Forest University who made my residence possible: Peter Kairoff, Kline Harrison, David Taylor, Jessica Francis among others associated with Casa Artom and Global Studies at WFU. The English Department at WFU, which has supported my work throughout, also deserves my profoundest thanks. The experience has enriched my life in so many ways.

Finally my family and my friends suffuse every poem I've ever written. They know who they are and have no need of naming. *Baci a tutti.*

A number of poems have appeared in the following journals:

"The flock of pigeons moves like a regiment," a sonnet from "The City Not Destroyed," *Southword Journal* 39, September 2020.

"San Trovaso," *The Honest Ulsterman*, June 2020.

"The Franciscan Hills," *Presence: A Catholic Journal of Poetry*, April 2020.

"Benchmark," *Voices in Italian-Americana*, 29: 2, 2018.

"The Pot of Basil," *The Tau: The Literary and Visual Art Journal of Lourdes University*, Fall 2018.

"Acqua Alta" *Prairie Schooner,* Summer 2018.

"Alla Bifora," "Fragment of an Ode," *Watchung Review,* Volume 2: July 2018

"Doubting Thomas," *The Anglican Theological Review,* 99.4: Fall 2017.

"*Madonna Lactans*," "The Painter's Riddle," *North of Oxford,* October 2017.

Rafts

to my mother and father

The water floods our lot
As it always does, though
This time it wasn't rising
From the pond and swamp
Below, but ran down
From the front, carving
Ravines in the yard, washing
Out the grass, trees and house.
All the landfill they had brought
To make the foundation firm.
The boulders along the driveway
Left standing, reminders
Of the bulldozers that first
Piled and levelled the dirt.
There you both stood
On what little remained,
Smiling, not understanding
That you would be swept away
Too, and here I would be
Alone, like an outcast
On a raft, who waits for help,
On waters as bereft as he.

Waking has been like learning to breathe
Without air, like living among elements
Foreign to us — sea caves and ocean deeps
Blind darkness and lambent surfaces —
And never finding safe harbor or landing.
Yet as the story goes, there are mountains
Where we may settle, reservoirs of culture,
Not ours, but recalling earlier days of travel
And somehow the grounds beneath us
Seem to be hardening, becoming familiar,
That once were deep in rebel territory.
Barbarous, adhering to ancient codes,
Colonial structures, paradoxes
Of our forefathers whose idealism
And presumption shadow us still,
As we wait to be swept away ourselves.
Here in this watery, phantom city
The daily iterations of our transience
Remind us to float on the lagoon,
Ready for any tremor or rising tide.
The weight of our buildings and beings
Shifting on the moments as they transpire.

The ubiquitous waves unite as they diminish.
The enduring trees branch out as they extend.
Metaphors for rootedness and movement.
One sinking or cresting throughout the islands,
The other struggling against the artificial.
There can never be a place where both
Are reconciled. Where root systems sway
Underwater as the trees grip the waves.
Where waves strike down into the seafloor
And never break, hanging like cooling glass
From a blowpipe between water and fire.
Like this darkly translucent glass horse,
Fixed and fluid, hind legs ready to jump.
An aqueous image of the delicacy
Of permanence, of how nothing lasts
And everything falls quiet, except
The present, which is always moving
Yet rooted deep. Time ungraspable
But the only form in reach, because
We can neither choose the trees nor waves.
We must rise like saplings in the spring
And ride the rivers flowing to the sea.

Torcello

Ruskin felt that in Torcello art
Was the first expression of a belief,
Beset and beseeching, from the threatened heart
By worshippers who sought refuge and relief,
That here lay the foundations for grand architecture,
The flowering of the stones of Venice, the world's
Center. Gothic art from gothic nature.
Our best and worst caught in sculpted curls
Of Adam, Eve, and Angel; in the serpent's mouth;
The triumphal Madonna; the universal judgment;
The meeting of East, West, North, and South;
The great painters and the descent to the decadent.
Torcello is surrounded by the original marsh.
The barbarians returned and floods are increasingly harsh.

Barbacane

Verona, November, 2018

The Bible is anchored only at one end,
Which we can't see. A cantilever so rigid
Its base is as deep as it must extend
To support a turret or a jutting upper floor.
A text in travail, like the Ego and the Id —
Forgive us for we know not what we do —
From the beginning to the close of the story.

The divine intrusion into the spiritual core
Is tangent to history, never passing through
Into reality, almost like Venice itself.
A feat of design based at first on fear
Becoming a need for conquest from its glory.
Elsewhere in Italy it was Ghibelline and Guelph.
And then we climbed to watch the stars appear.

Points of Trust

to Walter Balzano

The benchmark is meant to measure
Each side of any triangle
Down to the nearest millimeter.
In thousands of a distant angle
Toward the highest mountain we see.
The steadiness of the building where
The ground is sinking and the sea
Is rising. Along many *calli*, there
Is often the head of a marking nail.
The choice that established the points
Of trust — that never fail
To form the necessary joints
As from earth to sun and moon.
The future shimmering on the lagoon.

It must be driven deep to be strong
Never shifting, depending on another
Only when gauging those who belong:
Lover, sister, parents, brother,
Cousins, neighbors, the friend
Who accompanies the dying one
Not knowing when it will end,
But believing when it'd begun,
Like Dante, that it was immortal.

It is in the center of the Rose.
No matter how far, it's the pull
Of the door that will never close.
It is the nail in the heavy stone
That balances all that is known.

Madonna Lactans

Omai sarà più corta mia favella,
pur a quel ch'io ricordo, che d'un fante
che bagni ancor la lingua a la mammella.

[Shorter henceforward will my language fall
Of what I yet remember, than an infant's
Who still his tongue doth moisten at the breast.]
Dante, *The Divine Comedy, Paradise*

Somewhere on the edge of the inside
Of her loosened dress, the baby's suckling
Where Maria's clothes were once opened wide
And flowing milk paralleled Christ bleeding
From the cross, redeeming or giving wisdom
To those who fed as the infant had, until
After the religious wars and the Council
Of Trent forbade it even in supplication.
Before the Baroque, *The Tempest* of Giorgione
Has a mysterious nude nursing a child.
Eve with Cain? Virgin? Whore? As unknown
As the storm is: God's anger? The wild?
While we seek the Being who also needs us
Blesséd be the Breast that breastfeeds us.

Off center, her gaze as direct as his Venus is
Indirect, challenging as the scrutiny of Manet's,
Rude as Titian's in Urbino is seductive
Amid a rich interior, one not in Giorgione's
Venus, as Titian knew while finishing it
In Giorgione's enigmatic, poetic manner.
Soldier or shepherd looks at where they sit.
The infant aside reveals her pubic hair.
The riddle of *The Tempest* has led some
To view it as the first subjectless painting.
Perhaps we, the subjects, search for home
In this early *paesaggio* where we're lingering
Within a stormy landscape that still needs us.
Blesséd be the Breast that breastfeeds us.

The Painter's Riddle

Blue is the color of the distance
Leonardo said. Was he thinking
Only of the sky, or missing
Someone loved? Those changing tints
Of dark and pale blue draw the eye
To vanishing points behind the portrait
Or the sacred scene and suggest a place
And story, past or future, dimly lit,
That highlights the evanescent face,
The curls, the angelic knowing hints
Of joy and sadness, the painter's riddle
Of the foreground, of starting high
On the canvas rather than the middle,
And why blue is the color of the distance.

Oratory of the Crucifixion

On Giandomenico Tiepolo's Way of the Cross

In the Stations of the Cross, a pattern
Emerges, different from every angle,
Emphasizing the crucifixion
And so leaving little to learn
Beyond the pain and betrayal
Implicit in every scene.
The *Via Crucis* a mere spectacle,

Or tending toward the Ascension
And each fall and each rising,
Meeting the mother, Veronica's
Cloth, the spear, the blood that flows
Recalling the despised Son
Hopelessly caught between
Suffering's end and its cause,

Until the sun on the third day rose
Like the glass of Sainte-Chapelle.
Did Jesus think of his family
Or God, the third and last time He fell?
Their grief beneath the cross?
What He would never see:

The story the Stations tell
Balancing the gain with the loss?

In a room at the Church of San Polo
The audience takes glee in the world.
Its theater of cruelty, whip, and scourge.
Never understanding the text or the gloss
The nature of what was laid low
And rose with its banner unfurled.
Never feeling the urge

To look up and accept the purge
Of moral scrutiny when he arose
After the exhaustion of each of His falls.
Almost every spectator appalls
Giandomenico, who knows
The unfolding narrative crime
When Jesus fell the third time.

The Studio of St. Augustine

By Vittore Carpaccio was based
On *The Studio of St. Jerome*
By Antonello da Messina.
Both depict the early fathers
At work on their writing desks
Surrounded by the artifice
Of the Renaissance.
The ancient world's erased
But for emblems in each home.
They both are humanists
Weighing the spirit and law:
Jerome's lion with the thorn
He removed from his paw;
St. Augustine in his studio,
Ecstatic and forlorn,
Writing his saintly friend,
As Jerome appears in the light
To announce that he is dead.
Will he continue to write
What he will never send
And is already written and read?

Venice and the Trees

Walking
In this
Artificial
City
Is like
Walking
In another's
World,
Through
The light
Of sea
And sky.

Walking
In the woods
Is like walking
Through
One's
Consciousness.
Dark and
Subterranean,
Like the timber
On which
Venice rests.

Venetian Pastoral

Across from the golden tesserae of San Marco
A river flowed through a field where nuns
Grew their fruit, but now the river runs
Underground, swallowed as its name
"Rio Batario" submerges "rio."
Today San Marco square is still the same
As when the field and river disappeared.

The covered meadow absorbs the hidden streams
Until high tide when estuaries tend
To rise up with the sea and water bubbles
In flooded drains. A re-emergence feared
Where outdoor is designed to feel like inside
(As in your mind each piazza seems
A public room, where Art and Nature blend)
And land and water share each other's troubles.

The field was once a floodplain. Fish still glide
Through *aqua alta*. Even the orchard at San
Zaccaria, felled by the Doge, would later stand
As columns of the arcades whose arches fuse
Capitals and rows to feign a forest.

Every stone of Venice rings as Ruskin said
It should with its rustic origins. Nature's ruse
Is that it often rises from the dead,
From buried roots, as the river's unrest
Heaves in the ocean when it slowly dies,
Casting land as apples to our eyes.

Hypnerotomachia

This book of the strife of love
Should have been written in italics
Instead of the Roman lettering
Of Aldo Manuzio. Of
All books, it's most intimate.
Like a handwritten tale of conflicts
And mythological reconciling,
Deep in the woods, an ornate
Court with erotic underpinning
And veneer. Phallic archways
And invitingly purple passages.
Always in plural, it depicts
How design with content plays
To master the printing press.

Syntactical painting where syntax
Collapses into repetition, where
Grammar and word choice become
One and the same over and over
Again, where what comes in a dream
Is what's dreamt, where the facts
Presented are neither here nor there,
Where what isn't is what's deep,
Where the blind, the deaf, the dumb,
Remember what it was to see,

To hear, to speak. Not asleep
But waking, not knowing how to be
Haunted by what the senses discover
Having been an incarnate we.

Europa's confused, who wouldn't be.
She put the garland on the bull.
Her waiting women have disordered
Her dress, the bull is now licking
Her foot. The sky's visible between
The trees as she's carried disturbed
While the colorist adorns the picture.
The canvas is more than full
Tumescent to the point of bursting
There's no way a mortal could flee
Such an approach when both
The divine and the human collude
In the kidnapping and the rapture,
Even when brush and conscience are loth. . .

To describe what happens next
What violates the frame, the nude
Becoming the naked, the brutal capture
Tormenting the will, the insatiable text
Swallowing the word before the word
Is made flesh, now unforgivingly altered
Would be sacrosanct, the mythological
Forbids, while religion would unlink
The reliquary of opposites, which symbol
Yokes and metaphor points toward.

One may never know what to think
At such an entrance of the diabolical
Without grabbing and wielding the sword
Over the kneeling, all-powerful bull.

The Wells of Venice

Throughout the city in almost every campo
Great geometrical works of art, covered now
With thick metal lids. Children often
Climb them, lying across or sitting

At the edge. Their play over the years
Helps to erode the decorations. No one
Interferes. In the New World they'd be
Enclosed. Isolated as museum pieces.

They were devised to gather rainwater
In a city that is surrounded and infiltrated
By the salt sea so that Venetians could
Have "sweet" water to drink and to wash.

Many must wonder why these wells
Were so elaborately sculpted. The first
Idea of the city was safety. Its later aim art.
The wellheads seem to represent the soul.

Today with running water, they serve no other
Purpose than their purposeless beauty.
The lids are coffin-like, or like shields
Welded with a keen aesthetic eye,

Like Arabesque windows. Or like chimneys
Which proved a stonemason's apprenticeship
Complete. They are of another age and stand
In contrast to the clutter of our own,

Which either parodies us or leaves us numb
And lonely at the pretense of restoration
Or community, the loss of privacy,
In the drag of our deflating bubbles

Behind us on the streets whenever we seek
The growing crowd in our reborn downtowns,
Finding reasons for being among the bars
And restaurants that are learning to survive.

In Venice, we quickly value sight and being.
The full body climbing bridges and walking
Along the *fondamente*, *zattere*, the *calli*
Some so narrow you could pass the sugar

From window to window. Above the *palazzi*
The *altane,* high porches, are waiting
To be seen in the spectacle of seeing.
Squares of perspective against the empty sky.

Once in a while, a wellhead, a *pozzo* sits
As it was hundreds of years ago
For few pass and fewer yet ascend
Its sides. The sculpted flowers and designs

Almost as sharply defined as when first hewn.
They shine even whiter in the twilight
Like sacred vessels, baptismal fonts
Or *acquasantiere* inside sunlit churches.

Some stand forgotten. Weeds growing between
The cracks. Bases broken. Adornment faint
Or no longer visible. People pass by
As if they didn't exist. Sometimes someone

Often a visitor, will pause and look,
Survey the scene, consider, touch the stone
As if it were a wounded soul, whose fate
Had to be recognized before its end.

We're left to imagine when they were open
To the skies, accepting from on high.
Gathering water for the city to draw,
Gathering the neighborhood to their offering.

Then the artists who made them must have
Been glad to see them used as they were meant
To be used. Huge chalices of the republic
That made each citizen a cupbearer.

One familiar well is near the Gesuati
Church, behind which the Giudecca Canal
Is visible through the *sotoportego*
As if to say, here is the reason wells

Exist. The salt water no one can drink.
Today, the hot and humid air makes us
Crave water. The children on scooters race
Around the well and from bench to bench.

The beggars take a rest while everywhere
The pigeons strut, fly, or find their crumbs.
And the people gazing round notice
The well is still the center of the campo.

A blind eye with an ornate patch.
A soldier's shield that drains the water off.
A button set to light up the machine
Or better yet to finally shut it down.

Una vera da pozzo. Wedding ring and well
That in its era no animal could approach,
And which was only tapped at certain times.
The sky's purity kept fresh for drinking.

At those moments, if we can forget the noise
And distraction of our electronic world, we
Remember what we thirst for — full circle —
To replenish what was lost along the way,

Why we want order, enlightenment, and form:
To capture what is needed and to satisfy
Our senses. To lift them above their primal
Purposes of finding food and detecting danger.

The quality in nature that created
Our capacity for art, that helped build
This city out of the coastal marshlands
And linked the islands as we are linked

To something higher than ourselves, which
Haunts us as this city haunts all
Who must leave it, worrying they'll forget
The aspect that first had risen from the mud.

Regata Storica

These things never happened, but are always.
Sallust

Imagine the Greeks sailing along the steep
Impassable cliffs looking for a port.
They must have been relieved to find the deep
Harbor where today, engaged in sport,
Are four maritime republics (Amalfi,
Against Pisa, Genoa, and Venice).
Barbarism and civilization on the sea
Despite the cars, buses, the tourist's eyes
That rarely look upon it for the first
Time as did the settlers of the bay.
But an aspect must someway prevent the worst
Presumption from corrupting the scene. The lay
Of the land that formulates our dreams, the bird
Song from ancient fable that is still heard.

For here we are as though we'd never and always
Been, while heavy rains fall upon the race
Making the choppy waves a moving maze.
Again it seems that we are face to face
With what we forget and what remember
As we prepare to return to Siren land
On the other side of the peninsula, nearly summer.

Travelling much longer than we had planned,
Struggling not to give into motion sickness
As the car takes the many twisting bends,
We cover our sleeping daughter, whose dress
Is too thin for the air when midnight ends,
As deep into morning, night slowly extends,
And we fall under the spell of day's duress.

Cavallino

Caught between a leap
And slowly rearing back,
Of clear glass framing blue
That is a shade so deep
It shadows into black.
A luster smooth and soft
It tempts us each to touch
Then hold the horse aloft,
As it's best to never do
Or someday it will break
After a fumbling clutch
Or should the table shake.
The figure will not last.
The future shapes the past.

Il Libro D'Arte

This is a book of the folding of wisdom.
Beautiful, unique, an object of art.
An indivisible and incalculable sum
Stuffed with difference and falling apart.

This is Sofia's book. Today she drew
It. Her craft and design. The colors
Of her thoughts within a given time.
Pages green, red, lavender, and blue

Linked among Venice's rising waters
By the Grand Canal in the Guggenheim.
On the first page there is a sun and heart
On the second are clouds and a tower.

Sofia insists it describes our home.
That is her right. This is her art.
Just as she made a sun orange-yellow
Against a forest without drawing a dome.

The third's another heart with a window
Next to the window a square that's a blur.
The following one is a zombie and stairs
(A corpse in Denmark is strangely begotten.)

The undead arise from cavernous lairs.
Flowers grow below clouds made of cotton
And grains of rice spill when one opens to look.
What else could be in a marriage of book

And fine art, but a celebration of sorts?
The rest of the artwork is dark and abstract,
Styled like the last century's many resorts
To shelter from the explosions of fact.

Sofia knows this. She is wisely alive,
Though she cannot say it as she is only five.
So she draws and glues it together instead.
In most ways it is also over my head.

Dorsoduro

Le Zattere, the rafts, sitting at the edge
Of the islands, rock above the sea
As it rolls by. Leaving the boat
There's a moment of dizziness. The feeling
Follows you until it's normal to sway
In buildings, streets that themselves seem to float.
With no fixed place, time will disappear
As though space would. The vacancy revealing
The essence of what it means to be here
In the *sestiere* of the hard ridge
That in strong sunlight promises to stay,
But in low-lying parts floods to the knee.
The more beautiful, the more evanescent,
The more are the four elements blent.

Alla Bifora

Sparrows are both friendly and secretive,
Though the flocks of pigeons are more famous.
For they fill the Piazza and the *campo*,
Soiling the place, suddenly taking flight.
You wondered where the sparrows nest and live.
In hidden gardens, we thought, anonymous
Behind high walls, where we see wisteria grow.
Just as plates are cleared they quietly alight
And soon the noisy, sloppy pigeons come.
She felt sorry when a pigeon was torn apart
By a seagull with a killer's evil eye.
Nature has no conscience or it's dumb.
Sparrows are as cruel as brave and shy.
Humans no more moral than their art.

The sparrows are not part of the self-consciousness
Of Venice, its insularities and tangled
Side-streets. They care nothing for its dead ends
Or crowds of tourists, its dwindling residents.
They avoid being at the center. A drabness
Defines their colors. You'll find one oddly angled
Near untended shrubs where it easily blends
With the background. They have a sixth sense
That's necessary not to get lost in certain
Areas off the thoroughfares. In brief

They remind one of a type of man or woman,
The passerby Baudelaire describes in the city,
Moving at the edge, like beggar or thief,
Waiting for attention to lapse, the arrival of pity.

Rio Tera' dei Catecumeni

> *When Jesus therefore saw his mother, and the disciple standing by, whom he loved, he saith unto his mother, Woman, behold thy son!*
> *Then saith he to the disciple, Behold thy mother! And from that hour that disciple took her unto his own home.*
> 19:26–27 John, King James

Watching while the children raced
Back and forth we tacitly acknowledged
The catechism of the missing
And that with which it is replaced.
The second "r" in the word *terra'*
Moving the Venetian dialect
Toward the Italian language.
Standardized mistake, autocorrect.

The large paved *calle* it names
Where the underground canal is flowing
The presence that follows the children
Whenever a child has been chased
The parent who doesn't, another who claims
A child after a hard-hitting fall
Or a coat's been opened or removed
When the evening cold has embraced
The slowly emptying scene.

As darkness seeps into the grooved
Departures of the narratives,
The large clanging bells, the tall
Towers of *La Madonna Della Salute*
And the plague, the extinguished lives,
The health that returns for another day,
The parent who is not there, behind
The parent or sitter who is,
What's lost and someone else will find.

Throughout Venice, the many Madonnas
And *La Salute* on the highest dome
While Christ blesses from the lower one
Who dying gave her another son
Not James, not his brother.
The catechism of the deserted home.
The anguish of the abandoned mother.

The Mill or the Broken Houses

The dust of eight-hundred years
Never seems to stop circulating
In this house from the 1200s.
The floors are warped though they
Are made of stone. The cracks
Are telling signs of the fluid
Grounds on which the city rests.
In front of the house, a castellated
Brick wall rises up above our window.
Its warm brown reflection from late
Afternoon through the evening fills
Our rooms. In the back, smaller walls

Plot out the gardens of other houses
As diverse in period as they are in style.
The birds live there and at dusk bats
Hunt mosquitoes rising with the darkness
Through shadows outside and in.
Near the underpass of the mill or
The broken houses *(Sotoportego molin*
O de le case rotte), fit reminders of history's
Weight and grind, our apartment was built
While Venice was sacking Constantinople.
Its mother city. The dark Oedipal roots
Of society exposed like the stolen Horses
Of the Hippodrome in the glint of the sun,

Or like a totem pole among evergreens,
Or a wigwam that squats inside the inner
Circle of the village, deep in the woods
And the residing dangers. The sovereignty
Of nature is sublimated through ritual
Acknowledgement of its power, one that
Realizes how no one conscience can
Withstand its assaults unless a culture
And tradition inform it. Else Oedipus
Is abandoned to the savage world where
The individual is left in ignorance, unable
To fathom the encounter on the highway.

The dust that circles round us here
Separates the past from the future
And thereby makes the present seem
Like a ship, or better still, an island
Among islands disappearing behind us
As we sail away, so that each time
We (you from the Old World and
I from the New) return to either place,
For both are becoming home, though
Never at the same time or completely,
We cannot tell which is real. The line
Between them a faded architectural sketch.

To enter Venice requires no other
Starting place than the self that you leave
Behind as you travel in your separateness
And through its unreality, trying to describe
Its symbol of human aspirations to yourself,
As Marco Polo did to Genghis Khan,
And Calvino recalled in *Invisible Cities*.
As desire lays out the plans of the *sestiere*,
We are aware that any journey outward
Moves inward. The self that one escapes
Will resurface in the differences between
The human and the inhuman, the animal

And the divine. In every permutation
Of society and individual, of consciousness
And unconsciousness, which we may meet
On our way, Venice confronts us with faces
Of flesh and stone. Fetching and grotesque,
Iconic or mere semblances of such
That have been worn down by weather
And usage. Setting out to find them
They seemed hidden for our discovery
And created to describe a psychology
Of walking, a method loci for memory,
Sometimes monstrous, sometimes votive

Almost always passionate. Each walk
Bears a likeness of charity and art,
Hardship and dispossession. Thoreau
By Walden Pond or on Mt. Katahdin.
Dante with Beatrice or at the Arsenale
And thinking of the terrors of the *Inferno*.
The Jews who now return or those locked
In the first Ghetto, where they were born.
These figures mirror the reality of those
Fleeing to the lagoon for safety from
The invading Longobards who, unlike
Previous invaders, decided to remain,

And so blocked any passage back to
The *terraferma*. Thus Venice began
In the most improbable of places. Deep
Inside the self in the cleft cut by the
Devil's foot, redemption would have
To be sought and the human raised
From the marshy, threatening grounds
Where nature and culture meet, where
You and I have found a common home,
Our daughter too. Custom reconciling us
To our transitory life on these shifting sands,
Until we prepare to leave the rafts behind,

To return on planes like the cross masts
Of the earliest ships to navigate the oceans.
We are mystics who spin until we fall,
Assuming in our dizziness that we will find
The way to our colonial clapboard home.
An outpost in by now long-settled woods,
Where histories — primitive and civilized, wild
And secure — descend upon the unsuspecting
With the vengeance and curses of ancient tragedy,
Punishing the family lineage to its unhappy end.
The stage, our home, contrasts light and dark.
A *camera obscura* of what we understand.

Hippogryph

Jungentur jam grypes equis
[To cross griffons with horses]

On the canal side of the Palazzo,
        Hidden, barely seen,
There's a sculpture of Pegasus,
Whose hoof made the waters flow
On Helicon, the Hippocrene,
        Font of poetic inspiration,
Which lifts us, or turns us to stone,
As Medusa, the Gorgon, had done
To many before she was dead.
She whose hair became serpents
When she was raped in the Virgin
        Goddess's temple.
For one is human alone
        And pays for another's sin
        Whether or not he repents.
Pegasus still flies from the blows
        Dealt by Theseus
That severed Medusa's head.
Born of her blood, he created the springs
        From which all poetry flows,
And knows that its enchanting source
        Is as unbearable

As mating a gryphon with a horse
Is barren. And so Orpheus sings
    In a mesmerizing riff,
    Of the Hippogryph.

The Anonymous

Endure as testament to the Gothic craftsmen
Ruskin so celebrated. One can imagine them
With heavy wares thrown over their backs,
Their clothes still dusty from the last job,
Readying walls for the devotional bas-reliefs
That will remain nameless but catch the eye
Across the years and tell stories of Gospel
Travails and ecstasies, of saints and cities.
Great artists didn't create them. They make one
Think of artists going to the back of beyond
On horseback with paints, brushes, and easel
Hanging from their saddles, set to complete
A commission, a Crucifixion, a sorrowful
Or nursing Madonna, of those Byzantines
Deep in Calabria, where peasants still carry
Their belongings on their heads, who came
During a famine and portrayed their patron saint
Holding a basket brimming with loaves of bread,
Or of funerary objects from the ancient world:
Urns, decorated columns, sarcophagi, and gorgons,
Evil eyes, meant to frighten demons and death.
They remind us that the signing of artworks
Was not practiced for most of history, that
Artists disappeared and left at most a name
And the art itself. There are many churches

With not one painting or sculpture identified,
And works mistakenly attributed to a Master
In which only the maker's hand is apparent.
Perhaps they say more about us when we
Stand before them, the realized but anonymous.

Acqua Alta

In the shadow you cast
A pool slowly receding
As the high water withdrew.
Inside two crabs are still.
Many people have passed
Without stopping or seeing.

After moving your shadow
You ask if a local will
Put them in the sea
Before they're left to die
Deserted — high and dry.

When the Venetian seizes
The larger carapace
The mother crab's claws
Are lifted from its young
But there's a quandary:
Either hold the infant
Or protect itself.
It grasps the little one.

With memories of rain,
We are made to learn
That self-preservation
Is not the law of laws,
That waters return again
Toward the flooded drain.
A branch of the covenant
Damned and heaven-sent.

The Janissary

On a sunny day in the Christian East
Under the rule of the Ottoman Empire,
Turkish officials arrived to claim a boy
Ten years of age as a Janissary.
A soldier who would never be released,
Who would be raised a Muslim (rigorous sire
Of highly trained troops) in the employ
Of those to whom his parents were the enemy,
Whose eldest son had earlier joined the Crusades
To march for Christianity. The next would forget
His religion, as his brother had finally done
At the last of successive, brutal raids
In which he killed many before being slain,
Though memories of home and family would remain.

Once in a dream their lost children had met
On the battlefield, as son replaced son,
Until at last in 1453,
The boy now a man attacked Constantinople,
Saw its last emperor jump into the fray,
And became a lauded hero of Istanbul,
Making martyrs of those who did not flee
Or came to fight on that chosen day,
Melting slowly like salt into the sea.

Fragment of an Ode

Catullus wished he were the sparrow
Lesbia kept near her breast.
Such a thought comes like an arrow
And leaves no rest.

Here, each of us inhabits
The lover Catullus
For time is the sparrow
And Lesbia the space
To which the sparrow flits.

And both quickly forget us
Like Venice, her breast and her face.

The Pot of Basil

"O cruelty,
"To steal my Basil-pot away from me!"
John Keats, "Isabella; or the Pot of Basil"

Severing makes us remember and forget:
Ten years ago the heat never seemed to lift
As we lay beneath our draped mosquito net
And an old air-conditioner seemed a gift.
Now again, heat and the mosquitoes (always
Present, even in winter) are pestilential.
Only in late afternoon, a breeze plays
In the trees and over the body penitential
(Isabella suffering love and strife).
Out of nowhere, a bell rings and is done
In still air, another anomalous sign of life.
A shutter opens to the oblique sun.
In the Arab window there's a basil plant
To say I will and want to leave, but can't.

Doubting Thomas

Unbearably beautiful and unbearably sad
Is what I should have said when you complained
Of ennui, the affliction of youth, the half-fad,
As you slowly fell from childhood's sustained
Balancing act between the real and ideal,
Which made the future inexplicably dry
At the threshold. Seeing little appeal
Beyond wandering, you'd always irritably sigh.
Then, facing the sheer expanse of the real,
Like Satan gazing on the universe
Hanging in a chain, or Rafael sweeping
Through stars and planets, set to immerse
Himself in knowledge of the world, while keeping
Faith, you felt, as you packed your bags, an inkling
Of beauty and sadness, and so couldn't decide
What to do. There was the girl with the ring
In her nose and glasses. Time and tide
Made you admit that you were both too young
To last as a couple, but you weren't ready to go.
That is the gist of those folk songs you'd sung.

Then duty called and you went. A week or so
After, I saw her outside one of the churches
You'd loved. She who, like Christ's wound,
Was hesitantly touched — a ship that lurches
Before docking. Venice is now festooned
With tourists in nearly every neighborhood.
I wonder if later she sensed that you could —
If not believe — perhaps have understood.

Landings

There must be a deep awareness on the edge
Of consciousness, balanced between the object
And subject. It is how somewhere in the sedge
Earth and water combine, how mirrors reflect
What faces them and yet distort the appearance
Of the thing or onlooker that they contain,
How artists understand they create in a trance,
Or how from a sunny sky passing drops of rain
Send out circles in a pool or on a river
Standing or flowing as white clouds pass by.
It is like a memory that makes the body shiver
Or how one inherits an ancestor's gesture or sigh.
Laboring near death she managed to wait until
You came from the airport, and then the room was still.

She probably had something to say but wouldn't
Have remembered it, had she been able to talk.
It's like trying to represent what is most admired
In a place you soon have to leave. The more
Individual the phrase the better. A particular walk.
Perhaps not what you did but what you couldn't.
Those periods of peace you can't account for.
How on certain days when you were most tired
Your resistance dropped and you felt so content.

You reached for a figure of speech, a myth or a form,
But they only pointed beyond your comprehension.
You can't say what the intense experiences meant,
When the story's finished and when the song is done.
The coffin may be open, but the body's not warm.

So let's consult the map: a fish in the lagoon.
The streets as confused as they were where we've been.
Water makes it even more volatile,
More constantly mutable than the changing moon.
We know when landing we won't know where to begin.
For the pace will be too slow. Crowds in single file.
Losing the whole in the abstraction of the scene,
A face here, an ornamental window there.
Venice is never what someday it will mean.
For everyday it leaves itself in midair
As a boat bounces off a wave, or habit
Inures us to what we will pass through.
But time will come and tell us what to do.
One last look around and suddenly that's it.

Cupidity

At the library where you and I found solace
Away from evangelicals and decadents,
Between the Giudecca and a back canal, among
Those Ca' Foscari draws to its hidden *incrocio*
Not tourists but foreigners and Venetians
Who remain, while gondoliers come and go
Floating in the lagoon of capitalist outer space.
The cupidity that each of us somehow resents
Admits or exhorts. The repressed rancor of race
Coursing the internet to far flung
And intimate places. Perhaps the bindings
Of these books contain hope to locate
In sympathetic minds intricate findings
Of humanity before they're engulfed by hate.

The glare on the great painting of Tintoretto
In San Moisè is like the burning bush
In the desert, obscuring the familiar face
We seek with a deeper one we don't know
Which is closer to us, but under the hush
Of silence, a name left unnamed, a trace
On the tablet that in anger we would erase
And regret. For Jesus tells Judas what he
Thinks he has hidden — fear struck in his breast.

There's a dog in front of the wooden board
On which they eat. Peter will have to flee
Denying that he would later betray — blest
Only upon the cross, or dropping the sword
That severed the ear, caught in the glare of the Lord.

Somewhere at the origin of the Empires
Is the anti-colonial aim, the city
On the hill meant to shine toward Europe.
Once the warnings of invasions, the signal fires,
Pushed us toward the forest or the sea.
The next seclusion of our primal hope.
Before Venice the island of Torcello.
Ruskin's dream of a sacred genesis
In gothic nature before the wingéd lions
Raised their paws to hold a book and show
Pax tibi. . .with which the angel blesses
St. Mark on the marshes. Their word and wings
Testaments to the destroyed impulse. Signs
Made or given like tears in the nature of things.

Tears in mortal things. Neither an end
Nor a beginning but the changes of *Lachrymae*
Rerum flowing from one era to another,
From Virgil to Matthew Arnold. The ancients blend
With the moderns in uncertain, nervous play
Of intellect and sense. Where's the mother
Worship? The fire-lit caves where we sheltered
Gathering courage with belief? The heart
Is at the center of the brave and the quick.

The mind's a library that holds the Word
Before it's empty and echoes with a start,
Seeing that pitch darkness surrounds the wick
We finally light. Without the walls of the cave
The shadows are gone. The fire's all we can save.

So we pass the torch, carry the flambeau
And search again for a fortress in the sea
Or a refuge in the wilderness, far from
Zealots who threaten to overwhelm the city,
Barbarians gathering at the village gates,
Dragging us back like the ocean's undertow.
The like-minded seem almost deaf and dumb
Or unheard above the clamor. As the Fates
Decide who will rise and who will fall,
We are forced to cross the windy lake.
The hurricane lands and begins to stall,
Bringing floods and landslides in its wake.
But our uncharted lands must make us see
The various tides, the patterns of the tree.

The Fall of the Roman Colonies in the Veneto

When the storks began to lift their young
To abandon their nests, Attila the Hun knew
The siege of Aquileia was over. The assault
Prepared. Loathsome, dying cries were wrung.
The walls were overwhelmed, resistance through.
Pax Romana's order broken. What fault
But self-serving corruption caused the collapse?
The descending pattern of history is told
By those who escaped. Venice arose from the fall
Of Rome. The New World was born of the Old.
Fragile republics are finally caught in the traps
Of their own making. Cut off by a wall
They built for safety, they watch as the nests
Are emptied and the wave of soldiers crests.

The City Not Destroyed

Is often the one that will be occupied
Like the linked Venetian archipelago,
While the country is reduced to rubble.
(The targets were soldiers, much too long ago.)
In imagination, there is only one side
Unaffected by war's universal trouble.
When Silesia was shaken by the push and shove
Of warring Austrian and Prussian armies
It did not know the soldiers would be brothers.
When Nazis had to spare the beauty of Krakow
And Venice as their seat, bombing others,
They saw the cities as only meant for them.
Politics is war, waged to claim a gem
Bringing Christ and Europe to their knees.

In Krakow's medieval square, a trumpeter
Chimes the hour with a melody
Stately and kind, mostly secular,
But with an undertone of piety
That seems to capture time passing. One day
While a battle raged below his tower
Threatening the church from which he'd play
He grabbed his bugle and, amid a shower
Of arrows, warned of the attack. One stray
Pierced his throat before the song was done.

His memorial slowly gathers power
As it marks that day when he was shot.
The tune's performed until its interruption.
The precise end of every mortal lot.

The flock of pigeons moves like a regiment
Across a field in martial preparation,
But with a comic bobbing of the head,
The amorous gurgle of the males, the run
And flutter of individuals, legs oddly bent
Or missing, the occasional bird lying dead
Or eaten with ruined ruffled feathers. It's said
That they are knights, victims of a spell
Cast by a witch to tempt a greedy king.
The gold received he planned to take to Rome
To free the knights, but he forgot to tell
The Pope, or reach the city, finding home
Where he might indulge himself and sing
A drunken song to keep the pigeons swirling.

If only the Sea Remained

Imagine a city you once called home,
That large parts were destroyed in the war,
That tonight is the last night before
You face the shattered convent and dome.
Lost in the rubble of pounding blows
Of artillery and bombing every day,
The broken fountain that randomly flows.

Croce saw the planes as birds of prey
A storm gathering for the coming attack,
Their engines as loud as the siren's scream
As he sat safely on Sorrento's back.
Imagine you are afraid of sleep and dream
For tomorrow early you are returning
To see what stands in ruins still burning.

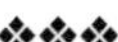

You are a conquering soldier who claimed
Pompeii, landing at a provincial port
And setting up camp in a nearby field.
The city has been and will be a resort,
But for now it is only the vanquished
Welcoming the assaulting liberator
Alive at least, if terribly maimed,
Swept up in the sadness of the wished
For, waiting as the wounds slowly healed,

Until conspirers no longer would whisper,
When they finally know what to do
And forgot the portions they'd stained
And that if only the sea remained
It would shimmer and still be blue.

Body and Blood

Scoured now, its scaffolding stowed,
The Rialto Bridge is bone white
As before *La Salute's* dome had glowed.

The parting ebb-tide has fully risen.
The sun that had set is at full height.
The nearest bridge once draped in plastic

Today permits our homesick sight.
Even to the same, the return is drastic.
It means we must recast this light

As Titian had depicting sin
In the Sacristy: *Cain and Abel,*
Isaac bound and the decollation

Of Goliath in a triptych fable
In which blind faith and heroism
Answer the anger of a jealous killing.

The founding blow is struck again
Though changed in Tintoretto's prism
Through miracle if God is willing.

The Wedding of Cana, water to wine.
The table dividing women from men
As Christ in a nimbus makes a sign.

Overwinter

Briefly back here again
I see at the twilight hour
Warmth in this southern state
Comes quickly to full flower.
A singing Carolina Wren
Signals the landing of spring,
But winter remains to be seen
In front of our North-facing house.
Where the tallest trees are bare,
While basking in light of the South,
The leaves in the backyard, opened,
Form a blind concealing the sky.
The seasons are changing between
The slant of dusk and my chair
Placed in the listing wind.
The sun and the shadows arouse
Azaleas and dogwoods to bloom.
Out of the cave's dark mouth,
Up in the strongest boughs,
The lives of the black bears resume.

Forest Communion

The toppled smooth-skinned tree
Forked in the middle with an apron
Of roses, hostas and liriope
Fell in the rain-soaked ground.

It is like a stricken body
Uprooted suddenly, without hope.
A dying victim of a hit and run
Hurricane that pummeled the town.

Our other trees stand guard
Like sentries fearing the next shot
Will ricochet across the yard:
Oak to hickory, dogwood to pine

Gripping tightly, resisting the rot
Vulnerable in the cultivated design
Subduing the randomness where roots
Branch out, dig deep, and intertwine

In a complex forest communion
Cradling the sick who have lain
In a clearing until raising shoots
Up to the sky struggling for the sun

Or under the ground battling for rain.
The beech tree stretched on the earth
Releases a history of plane upon plane,
Forsaken it seems, forgiven for birth.

Native Green

When we depart the hard and lambent light
Of Venice, its canals, suspended palaces
Reflected skies, circling shuttered night
That keep the city floating like the chalices,
Miraculous crosses, views above the roofs
In medieval quest for saintly, virgin power
To return the body to bread, wine to water,
To refine the icons, liturgy, disdain all proofs,
Which has dimmed with every passing hour
And religious war that wreaked a world of slaughter,

You'll miss the decadent embellished arches
Almond eyes in profile — Arab windows —
Feel the *tramontana* as it marches
Down the Alps into the lagoon
Rue the cold that sharpens cooling shadows
And makes the *campi* no longer seem a home
Whose rooms are brightened by the sun and moon.
While steadying myself, gazing at the scene
To realize the clandestine nature of the poem,
I'll close my drapes of deeply native green.

White Birch Epiphanies

La Befana vien di notte
Con le scarpe tutte rotte.
[The good witch called Befana
Comes at night with broken shoes.]

The end of the Nativity story.
Thirty-one years since his death,
The snow-bound Epiphany
That captured the fleeting breath.

Far off with the good witch
Seeking the Christ-child still
Who carries the bait and switch
Of candy and coal to fill

The good and bad child's stocking.
Ugly, but posing no danger,
She housed the Magi to bring
Spices and gifts to the manger.

A story becoming a rumor
That drove her in yearly searches
To find Christ as we would the tumor
And beauty of snowy white birches.

They live for over a century
But away from the woods may grow
For only some thirty years.
The painting allows us to see
The cast of their shadowy glow
As every Epiphany nears.

Bathed in Red

Unde Origo Inde Salus. [Salvation is in the Origin.]

On the roof of the Fondaco dei Tedeschi
You can imagine Venice's many churches
By the tilting campaniles, and see
That art and religion had the greatest purchase
On life in this most practical of cities.

Once a frescoed market, storehouse and dwelling
It is now a high-end mall for the flow
Of consumers in decades of abandoning
An ancient artistic past for the silk purse
Of Western style — without content — who show
How on seven continents and seven seas
Computer gadgetry and high-rise commerce
Release Tintoretto's flying bodies.

Fearing the phone will cease to ring
(The theme of our lives is a mobile phone)
Or have a tone no one recognizes
(Saying we're not when we are alone)
The faithful even have a special door
As in groups they file near the Rialto.
Such devotion: to work even more
With less and less time, in a place
Ephemeral by nature, apocalyptic in origin.

Tonight the Salute was lit in smoky red,
Dressed in red velvet inside, for
The suffering of the world. The Madonna's face
And gestures bid Venice pray for sin
And plague to be driven hence. Prayers
For the living, answers for the dead.
Help for the suffering of the church
Was written in purple neon across
The cupola, where stone saints and angels perch
Perilously above history and the loss
Of those not saved. While water climbs the stairs
Celebrants hope the hour is theirs,
However profane and filled with the crush and hum,
With floating balloons and candles priced for prayers,
That the material mystery would someday come,
The miracle cure, and catch them unawares.

As to Mary came the dove of the annunciation
From the origin of Venice came salvation

It was the first day of the Christmas fair
In Budapest, handcrafts by Hungarians
Like the book in which I'm writing
On my plush mass-manufactured chair,
Thick-papered, hand-designed, green
Leaf and copper tendrils, sewn binding,
Tactile, imperfect. By original artisans
Whom capitalists may undersell, but who in turn
Build what creates self as it's produced.

At an early age, they begin to learn
What careful hands can do, so value craft
In a culture where what's made and seen
May be pre-modern, but proves one's used
To working well. Homo sapiens
More active than passive on a broken raft
Subject to rising waters of the industrial world.

Along the flooded, stormy shorelines of alien
Futures, the keyboard, paintbrush, chisel, and pen,
The swirling trade winds that steadily hurled
Us, delivering goods to distant, foreign lands,
Were never moved solely by mortal hands.

What do we want? The hour has not come,
With Christmas shops and churches bathed in red,
To comprehend the opposable, turning thumb
Or prayers for the living as answers for the dead.

San Trovaso

How could I forget? For it would be
Like forgetting myself just after I'd found
The words, music and painting of an interior me,
An unfinished portrait in black ink and sound
But forget I did for almost three years.

Like weather that comes too late and deceives
I often dismiss the "I" and all its tears
But when I couldn't, I went to San Trovaso
To haymaking and the recovery of thieves
Understanding how, after reading *Tintoretto:*
Tradition and Identity, this *Last Supper*
Much disliked by Burckhardt and Ruskin
Could be read as tragic-comic genius,
That the drunken man grabbing the wine jug
Is mirroring the miracle of Jesus,

Of the body and blood, that all the stir,
The sense of betrayal, the tumultuous sin,
Around the haloed holiness, was meant to tug
At those sharing the table, to whom the gesture
Was too magnificent, was beyond any finding

They had ever made, that all was a blur,
That it would be enough not to forget
What happened by describing it, that the blinding
Light could only be remembered if it was set
In stone, paint, and on paper for all to return to

As I've often done to the parish church
Almost unmapped, not often passed through
By the crowds trailing an unconscious search
For the dialect of the self, to learn and to teach
Despite memory's undiscoverable breach.

Casarlano

> *Presepe, presepio*: The term derives from the Latin *praesaepe*, i.e. crib, manger, but also an enclosure where sheep and goats were kept.

The village is busy with its own affairs:
Blacksmith, baker, a potter mending porcelain,
Mason, butcher, cheesemaker, all of the wares
In this studious Neapolitan tableaux.
A *presepe vivente*, this Bethlehem
On a hilltop town above Sorrento.

As the audience, the viewers, walk the lanes
Built from storehouses and sheds almost the age
Of the era they depict, of Mediterranean
Vintage, which, modern and mechanized, remains
The ancient world fixed upon a stem
Of roots deeper than the Bible story itself.
Here the houses challenge the mountain shelf.

For behind the public noise of this stage
Fumes of the donkey, the cow, the horse, the sheep
Rise with livestock rustling in narrow pens
With barely enough room to eat and sleep.

Human traffic is observant as only the beast,
The pulse of the deity (lacking familiar language),
The winter smell of the earth, the living heat
Of animal enormity rules and extends
Beyond the measure of the most and the least.

Above in the orange grove the fruit now fills
And hangs heavy like a Christmas tree.
The *presepe* artists, to describe the holy scene
Must include the landscape, the rolling hills,
The grotto, the Roman ruins, and set between
The columns, Mary and Joseph, the Christ-child,
While on a road outside a broken wall
(The passion in the garden, the agony)
The traveling Magi herald the unreconciled,
That the star that falls will never fall.

Not even Christmas Eve, infant displayed
In the manger, after hay has been spread,
Dried in the crèche, the crib has been made,
The golden halo shines round his head,
The spices and gifts have been carefully laid,
Not when the beasts have circled and gone to bed.

The shepherds play their music as the baby is tucked
Between the world we inhabit, the one we construct,
Comet, asteroid, or lightning struck.

After Virgil

(*The Aeneid*, Book I, 538–543)

After swimming we arrived here on your beach.
What kind of men are these? What country allows
A barbarous custom that denies as we beseech
The hospitality of the sand, the fruit of the plows,
Which declares war on us and forbids respite
On the nearby land. If not in the human race
In the fraternity of mortal arms that embrace,
Then at least believe in the gods, whose sight
Remembers the just, the unjust man and place.

The trouble is those seeking refuge are Trojan.
Soldiers who later conquer Italy (though landing
In what now is Sicily). This loose translation
Clearly expresses a mixed feeling. Seen
In light of those refugees drowning in seas
That are the same as those Aeneas sailed
After the defeat in Troy, seven years these
Men sought rest on many shores and failed.
Finding land they would someday aim to seize.

If only by numbers the land they sought was theirs.
They came for a coastal dwelling and spread beyond
The woods that lined the shore. Wanting more than shares
Of hunting and gathering, they broke their word and bond

What else could be expected? Their right was sheer
Might, weaponry learned in defeat, strength in suffering.
The skill to put dread in the enemy comes from fear
Once felt. Can pity for the defenseless ever bring
An end to conquest for those seeking refuge here?

Nature Morte

Art is an anatomy of how decay
Thins the corpse to feather and bones,
Renders how ripe the fruit must be,
How wings are spread to fly away,
Outlines visions of other zones
From those we travel. Skeleton
Journeys only on the map.

Seeing the desiccated body
Of the bird, you thought of paintings
Throughout Oplonti and Pompeii.
Post-modern, classical figuration
Of branches and leaves, of a delicate wrap
Over a bowl of figs, which clings
Yet is transparent. Musical cupids
Without floors, but three-dimensional.

Though realistic, such fine art warps
Reality by seeming to float
Without reference points. Unfixed
The bird's beak hangs ready to call
For release from its crumbling corpse.
One searches in silence for the note
It sings among the singing birds.
A still life dead to action and to words.

Benino's Dreams

Paradise is a dream guided by consciousness
Where one escapes the collapsing elevator
And heads out to the rooftops to witness
The city streets, distant mountains, the skater

On the park's frozen pond, alone before
The others come, who skillfully cuts the ice
In figure eights, overlapping circles. Or
It's summer and the hallucinogens of paradise

Are blooming everywhere. One sits among
Them in a daze, for flowery dreams are flowing.
Rooftops become the grassy grounds, the tongue
Speaks many languages and can sing

Of fragrances wafting us to the coast
Where a thousand sailboats fill the horizon
And the body warms like morning toast
In a gentle ever-shining sun.

When one needs a change of mood or scene
It's done before the feeling is a thought.
Snow swirls into a moonlit screen
Upon which one's many days are wrought:

First childhood, first love, without pain.
Prescience, memory, future, present, past
All at once like rivers and falling rain
From ocean to ocean. The sky moving, cast
In mirrors, a monument whose hue and form
Change with the weather — calm or storm.

But we know that wish-fulfilling change
Is not enough, that the storm breaks limbs.
The calm's foreboding. The mirror shatters. Strange
Weather moves across the mountains, dims
The sun when least expected. What if this
Is what is wanted most? The bitter cold
Of disparate words and days. Consciousness
That labors to continue, uncontrolled,
Plummets though the ice, gasps for breath.
Irreparable, the elevator stops,
The buzzers sounds, hurtles to our death.
What if soldiers trample through the crops,
While Benino dreams of someone from afar
In hope and dread beneath a warning star?

The Madonnas of Bellini and Donatello in Boston

There's a crisis that's difficult to place.
An unease in both mind and body
Politic. You see in the gesture and face
From many sides unsettling anger and glee
At the thought of suffering or fear
That might be inflicted on the enemy.
For during this long tumultuous year
Are we leading or are we being led?
Like those on the road
To Golgotha who place the crown on His head
And scoff, "Save yourself! King of the Jews!
Son of God!" and repeatedly goad
Him whenever He falls, we have few clues
As to what has happened or will happen.

Veronica. The Madonna, the women and men
Stand uncertain at the cross when Jesus dies,
Heavy compassion and grief at the pain
Expressed by the various cast of their eyes:
The anonymity, which like a secret will remain
Forever in the cloth, a bloody icon,
The mystery overlooked for the sake
Of Barabbas and the fervent need to fight on.

It's in the stricken face of Bellini's mother
As if she saw a soldier drive in a stake
Who gently holds her baby and almost weeps
At the knowledge that's too much to smother
Both their sacrifices welling up as He sleeps.
Divine and human, worshiped and defiled.
A despised and rejected man, born with the child.
While Donatello's sculpted *Madonna of the Clouds*
Looks away, foreseeing or recalling His fate.
Her ample dress both mother and baby enshrouds.
Queen of Heaven haunted by summoned hate.

Human malfeasance and malevolence are often
No more than human frailty. Think of the heist
We all understand, but not the murderer when
It's cold and cruel. Revenge is what's sacrificed.
All the despised and rejected are Christ.

The Franciscan Hills

Does something outside hold the self still
Or is it the force of the journey leading me
To acknowledge the umber, the earth-toned hill,
The green respiration where I'll find
The woods of New England, Dublin City,
The Bay of Naples, San Francisco, child's play
In White Plains, Venice thrice, now today
The small city on the edge of Appalachia?
The contemplative calm, the patient mind
That all too rarely kindles into rapture.

As it did this morning in the cancer ward
Among the balding heads, sheer exhaustion.
A rising beatitude, a resounding chord,
Grace that moves beyond the hope of cure.
Like standing on a cliff with the wind
Behind stronger than anyone can endure.
Echoing through the abyss and empty sky,
The moving air of mutual recognition
Like that look from the outcast driving by
Who waved hesitantly, not knowing if
I'd greet her. Sitting on the front stoop, I
Hoped she had seen me when I finally did.

A look that is a testament of kinship.
A canticle of sister moon and brother sun
That binds us to the animals and birds.
The naked saint who scorns his father's riches
And later builds a chapel in the field.
Roaming made walking be his words.
The Five Wounds of St. Francis never healed.

Saint Anne

Below the mountainous heights of Sorrento's
Sprawl is a marina dedicated to Saint Anne
Between promontories where one road slows.
A village made for neither God nor man
That is hard pressed by the cliff-face above.
Fishing nets and sightseers fill the harbor
While docks protrude like fingers of a glove.
An empty Russian-owned villa is its neighbor.
The tourist haunt looms on the high plateau.
Somehow the vaulted church with bright majolica
Tiles resists the threats behind and below,
As mother and daughter share the Ave Maria
On the high altar of the spiraling inlet
That we may have our intercessors yet.

www.ingramcontent.com/pod-product-compliance
Lightning Source LLC
LaVergne TN
LVHW020652100826
845148LV00012B/2443